Dirty, Loud and Brilliant

Join Carol Vorderman in *Dirty, Loud and Brilliant* and discover how to make bottles sing, light a torch with a lemon, make a fire extinguisher – and many other mind-boggling things. There are masses of easy to follow experiments, all of which you can do using materials you'll find around the home.

Science has never been so much fun, so make yourself a Rainbow Drink and have a Dirty, Loud and Brilliant time!

About the author

CAROL VORDERMAN was brought up in North Wales. She has an Honours and a Master's Degree in Engineering, and has worked on various engineering and computer projects. She first appeared on television as the Numbers Expert on Channel 4's 'Countdown' programme. Since then her television and radio experience has expanded enormously, including BBC Television's 'Take Nobody's Word for It' and ITV's 'Wide-Awake Club'.

Carol lives in Yorkshire and London. *Dirty, Loud and Brilliant* is her first book.

DIRTY, LOUD AND BRILLIANT

CAROL VORDERMAN

Illustrated by Larry Wilkes

KNIGHT BOOKS
Hodder and Stoughton

Text copyright © Carol
Vorderman 1988
Illustrations copyright © Hodder
and Stoughton Limited, 1988

*First published in Great Britain in
1988 by Knight Books*

Printed and bound in Great
Britain for Hodder and Stoughton
Paperbacks, a division of Hodder
and Stoughton Limited, Mill
Road, Dunton Green, Sevenoaks,
Kent TN13 2YA (Editorial Office:
47 Bedford Square, London
WC1B 3DP) by Richard Clay
Limited, Bungay, Suffolk.
Photoset by Rowland
Phototypesetting Limited,
Bury St Edmunds, Suffolk.

British Library C.I.P.

Vorderman, Carol
  Dirty, loud and brilliant.
  1. Activities for children
  I. Title   II. Wilkes, Harry
  790.1'922

  ISBN 0-340-42619-5

This is for my Mum, Jean, whom I love very much.

Introduction

If you want to be dirty, you want to be loud
You can jump in a puddle, you can scream in a
   crowd.
But if you want to be brilliant and utterly wow
Then read this book well – it will show you how.

How to be brilliant is quite easy you see
You must learn to ask questions and try hard to be
Completely nosy when you try out the tricks
Why does this work? Is this a fix?

How do submarines sink and then float again?
Light from a lemon? Just use your brain:
Make rockets in your bedroom, make the best that
   you can
Watch popcorn explode, make toffee in a pan.

Try harder and harder, be dirty and loud
Sing it from the rooftops, be different from the
   crowd.
Be utterly brilliant, be utterly wow
It won't take you long, so start right NOW.

Carol Vorderman

Contents

9

WET FINGERS AND HEAVY GLASSES

THE 'STUFF YOU NEED' BIT

Two glasses

Water

Pencil or pen

A small piece of wood, or a ruler

THE 'WHAT TO DO WITH THE STUFF' BIT

Make something that looks like weighing scales, with the pencil in the middle, the ruler on top of it and the glasses at either end nearly full of water. Nudge one glass towards the middle until the scales are almost balanced. What do you think will happen if you put one finger (dirty or clean, it doesn't matter) into the glass of water which is up in the air, but you don't touch the bottom of the glass? Does the glass

e ruler goes down. →

11

become heavier or not? It seems to, because the scales change. Stick your finger in the other glass, and the scales change again. Clever, huh?

THE 'HEY BRILLIANT, IT WORKS' BIT

Try using two or three fingers. When do the scales start to tip over? Put your finger or fingers in slowly and mark on the outside of the glass where the water is when the scales start to topple.

THE 'O.K., HOW DOES IT WORK?' BIT

Have you noticed that when you get into the bath, the water level goes up, and sometimes if it's too full it flows out over the top? About two thousand years ago, a bloke living in Greece, called Archimedes, noticed just that. He was so excited that he jumped out of the bath and ran down the street to tell his friend. The only problem was he had forgotten to put his clothes on and his bare bottom was showing – poor Archimedes . . .

Anyway, he also noticed that if you put an object (apples, wood, fingers or anything) in water, the object experiences an upthrust (a force upwards) which is equal to the weight of the water which it has displaced (pushed out). Now, by plunging your finger into the glass, the level of water is raised: your fingers experience an upthrust (a force upwards) equal to the weight of water which they have displaced. But if there is a new force upwards on your fingers, there must also be a new and equal force downwards on the glass – so the weight of the glass has increased by an amount equal to the weight of the water which your fingers have displaced. The more fingers you dip in, the more water you displace, and the greater the new weight of the glass.

12

Boats on the sea, goldfish in a tank and swimmers in a pool all do exactly the same thing. They all increase the weight on the bottom of the sea, tank or swimming pool floor by an amount equal to the weight of the water which they have displaced. If you don't believe me do this wet experiment again.

WET APPLES AND JUICY MELONS

THE 'STUFF YOU NEED' BIT

Measuring jug with fluid ounces (pints) on the side

Water

Apples, bits of wood, corks, strawberries, anything

THE 'WHAT TO DO WITH THE STUFF' BIT

All right then, you've got all the stuff in the list. Can you tell me how much the apple weighs only using those things? Think about it first before you carry on.

The answer: Half fill the jug with water, and make a note of how many fluid ounces of water are in the jug. Add the apple, which will float, and make a note of the new water level. The difference between the two levels gives you the weight of the apple. Check it by weighing the apple on the kitchen scales.

Water level rises.

THE 'HEY BRILLIANT, IT WORKS' BIT

Try weighing some other things which float, and check your answers on the weighing scales. The answers will be right. Then try things which sink – like magnets or stones. The answer will be wrong.

So using the jug only works with things that float. If you can't fit the apple into the jug, then get a bigger container, put it into an even bigger container, and fill the first one to the brim with water. Put the apple into the water, and some of it will spill over the top. Pour the spilt water into the measuring jug, and the number of fluid ounces it weighs is also the weight of the apple. Melons and cucumbers and oranges all float by the way, so does this book until it gets soggy!

THE 'O.K., HOW DOES IT WORK?' BIT

O.K., it works like this. A pint of water is equal to twenty fluid ounces, or put another way, a pint of water weighs twenty ounces (one pound and four ounces or 567 grams). Now, when you put the apple into the jug of water, the level of the water goes up, just like when you get into the bath. If the object floats, then the weight of water which it displaces is equal to the weight of the object. So the difference in water levels gives the weight of the object.

A cork floats with most of its body sticking out of the water, it only displaces a small amount of water, which shows that cork is quite light. An apple has about half of it sticking out, so it's heavier than cork – which we know. An orange, although it floats, just peeps out of the top of the water, and so that is heavier again. You can see that by your results. If you did the same experiment with objects that sink, you'll have discovered that they don't follow the same rule. (See **WET FINGERS AND HEAVY GLASSES** for more of the same type of thing.)

HOW TO CONFUSE A COCKEREL

THE 'STUFF YOU NEED' BIT

Water

Salt

Glass

Egg

THE 'WHAT TO DO WITH THE STUFF' BIT

Put an egg into a glass of water, and it will sink. Put about three heaped tablespoons of salt into another glass of water. It helps if the water is warm, because the salt dissolves better. Put another egg in the salty water and it will float.

Now to confuse the cockerel! Fill a glass half full of salt water, float an egg in it so that the egg doesn't touch the bottom of the glass. Then, very carefully, pour fresh water

17

on top but don't let the two types of water mix together. The egg is now floating right in the middle of the glass.

THE 'HEY BRILLIANT, IT WORKS' BIT

So, it looks like the egg is floating in the middle of a normal glass of water, but we know better. If you have trouble pouring the fresh water on top of the salt water, try pouring it slowly over the back of a spoon. Add food colouring to the fresh water and you will be able to see the two layers more clearly. (The coloured water should remain on the top, of course.)

THE 'O.K., HOW DOES IT WORK?' BIT

If you're like the cockerel – confused – then, here's how it works. Lighter liquids will always float on top of heavier liquids – as long as you haven't stirred them together – oil floats on water, for instance, and cream rises to the top of the milk bottle.

Fresh water is lighter (less dense) than the egg, so the egg sinks. Add salt to the water and things change, the water is now heavier (denser) than the egg, and the egg floats. When you pour fresh water on top, it floats above the salty water quite happily. The egg is now floating in the middle of the glass and no matter how much of each type of water you put in the egg will always float where the layers of water meet.

In the Middle East there is a sea called the Dead Sea which is full of salt. In fact, it has so much salt in it that fish can't live there (which is why it's called the Dead Sea). There are quite a few holiday resorts around the Dead Sea and because the water is so heavy it makes swimmers float really well – just like the egg. Apparently, if you lie in the water it's just like lying on a lilo and you can float around reading books without getting them wet. Weird, eh?

RAINBOW DRINKS

THE 'STUFF YOU NEED' BIT

Lemonade, ginger ale, blackcurrant cordial, squashes, milk shakes, ice cream: anything gooey and good to drink

THE 'WHAT TO DO WITH THE STUFF' BIT

So you want a sweet, gooey, lovely rainbow drink, huh? Well then, you have to experiment and this time I'm leaving it all up to you. The clue is to put the heaviest layer of drink at the bottom, followed by a lighter layer, then an even lighter layer and so on, with the lightest layer right on the top. Start with something like blackcurrant cordial and end with ice cream. If you find that they mix up inside the glass, pour the liquids in gently over the back of a spoon and you will be able to control them better. If you're careful, all the layers will remain separate, making a real rainbow drink.

THE 'HEY BRILLIANT, IT WORKS' BIT

If you're dead clever, then you will be able to make one using all the colours of the rainbow which are red, orange, yellow, green, blue, indigo and violet. See if you can do it. Mind you, you might get some funny tastes. A little tip is to try two of them in a separate glass before you add another layer, then if you go wrong you won't spoil what you've done so far. You could float cherries and bits in it as well, and see which layer they settle on.

THE 'O.K., HOW DOES IT WORK?' BIT

O.K., you feel a bit sick after drinking all that, but how does it work? Well, some liquids are heavier (denser) than others. So a glass full of one liquid – say, blackcurrant – will be heavier than the same glass full of water. Just like corks float on water, liquids float or sink too, and that's what you see in the rainbow drink: liquids floating on top of one another. The heaviest one is at the bottom and the lightest one is at the top.

In exactly the same way, cream rises to the top of a bottle of milk. The creamy part of a bottle of milk has a lot of fat in it, and this is lighter than the more watery part of a pinta, so if you leave it overnight it will rise to the top.

FUNNY FOUNTAINS

THE 'STUFF YOU NEED' BIT

A couple of bottles

Water – hot and cold

Salt

Small bit of card

Ink or food colouring

THE 'WHAT TO DO WITH THE STUFF' BIT

Here are two ways to make fountains. The first one's really messy, so make sure you're by a sink. Make up a jug full of salty water, adding as much salt as you can. Fill one bottle with the salty water, and one bottle with coloured fresh water. Make sure that they are both full to the brim. Put a card over the top of the bottle of salty water, turn it upside down quickly and put it on top of the other bottle; slip the piece of card away. The coloured water will burst out into the top bottle making a funny fountain.

The other way is to fill a fish tank or a big container full of cold fresh water. Next make up a little bottle of coloured hot water (an empty ink bottle would be great), cover it with a piece of card and lower it into the big container. Take the card away and watch the fountain grow.

22

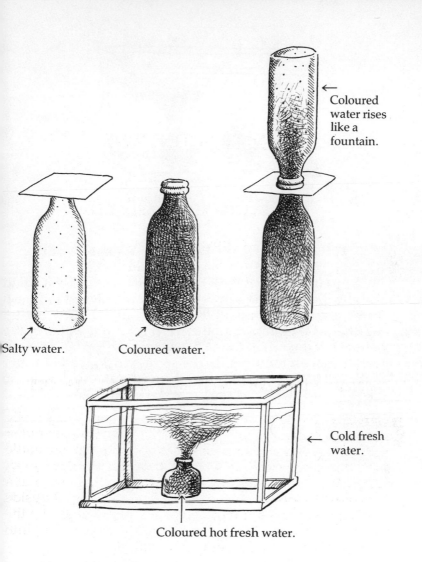

Coloured water rises like a fountain.

Salty water.

Coloured water.

Cold fresh water.

Coloured hot fresh water.

THE 'HEY BRILLIANT, IT WORKS' BIT

Try doing the second trick again, but fill the big container with salty water. Then lower two bottles, one with cold coloured fresh water, and one with hot coloured fresh water, and see which fountain grows fastest.

23

Cold salty water.

Coloured cold fresh water.   Coloured hot fresh water.

THE 'O.K., HOW DOES IT WORK?' BIT

Well, just like with **RAINBOW DRINKS**, the lightest liquid will always rise to the top. Salty water is heavier than fresh water and so it sinks. When you put the two bottles together in the first trick, the fresh coloured water in the bottom is lighter than the salty water in the top bottle and it rises to make a fountain. In the second trick, the hot water in the ink bottle is lighter than the cold water in the jug, so take the card away and the hot water grows like a volcano.

PLASTICINE PUDDINGS THAT FLOAT

THE 'STUFF YOU NEED' BIT

Water in a container

Plasticine

THE 'WHAT TO DO WITH THE STUFF' BIT

Work a piece of plasticine into a ball shaped like a small
Christmas pudding, and drop it into the bath or a bowl of
water. It will sink like a stone.

Now shape it into a boat and it will float. Slowly fill it with bits and pieces (anything will do), and watch how it goes lower in the water. Eventually, when you've loaded it enough, it'll sink.

THE 'HEY BRILLIANT, IT WORKS' BIT

It always seems odd when something floats one way and not another. The plasticine still weighs the same but the shape is different. So now we know that the shape makes it work, try making different shapes. Try making thin sides to the boat and give it a heavy bottom. Does it matter where you put the 'cargo'? If you put all the weight on one side, will it sink sooner?

THE 'O.K., HOW DOES IT WORK?' BIT

The Greek man Archimedes has been up to his tricks again. If you've already done **WET APPLES AND JUICY MELONS,** you'll know that the weight of the water which a floating object displaces is equal to the weight of the object itself. When the plasticine is in a ball, it sinks because a solid 'ball' of plasticine is heavier than the same 'ball size' amount of water. So to make it float, you've got to make a bigger shape, like a boat. The plasticine still weighs the same but it weighs less than a 'boat size' amount of water and it floats. Once it floats, mark on the side of the jug where the water level is, change the shape of the boat, float

26

it again and the water level will be exactly the same as before.

Now, when you add the 'cargo', the boat becomes heavier, it starts to go deeper into the water, and the water level on the jug will go up. This is exactly the way that ships work. They sail a lot higher when they're empty than when they're full, just like your plasticine boat. But again like the plasticine boat, they can only hold so much cargo before they sink.

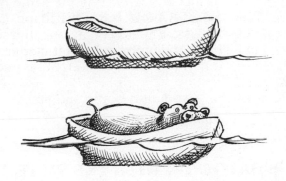

BUBBLE BALLETS (FIRST BIT)

THE 'STUFF YOU NEED' BIT

Washing-up liquid and water

Jug

Clean washing-up liquid bottle and straws

Glycerine – optional

THE 'WHAT TO DO WITH THE STUFF' BIT

The very first thing to do is make a magic bubble mixture. Put ten cups of water into a big bowl or jug and then pour in half a cupful of washing-up liquid. Stir it up with a spoon, trying not to make any bubbles.
Add about five tablespoons of glycerine to the mixture and stir it all over again.

Make a bubble pipe using a straw. Make four cuts about two centimetres long at one end of the straw, then splay it out like flower petals. Dip it into the bubble mixture, shake off the excess mixture and blow very gently to make lots of bubbles. You may have to shake the straw to free the bubbles.

A super brilliant bubble pipe can be made from a washing-up liquid bottle. Cut the flat end off the bottle, and make about ten slits between one and two centimetres long at the cut off end. Splay the slits out like flower petals, as before. Dip the bottom end of the pipe into the mixture and blow steadily. It may take a little time to get used to the proper breathing with this pipe: one of the key things is not to breathe in through your mouth. To release the bubble, jerk the bottle to one side.

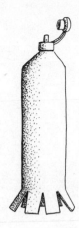

THE 'HEY BRILLIANT, IT WORKS' BIT

Try making all sorts of bubble pipes out of pieces of wire. See what strange shapes you can make. Try making a cube out of wire and dip that in the mixture – it should work.

If you wear woollen gloves the bubbles won't burst when you pat them, and so you could play bubble tennis.

THE 'O.K., HOW DOES IT WORK?' BIT

If you run the tap quickly you may have noticed that bubbles are formed on top of fresh water but they quickly disappear. To make sure that they stay, we add washing-up liquid. The washing-up liquid destroys what's known as surface tension, and it allows the surface of the water to be stretched into bubbles which form when you push air into the washing-up mixture. The glycerine is quite sticky and makes the bubbles last longer.

If you want to do more exciting tricks then look up **BUBBLE BALLETS (SECOND BIT)**.

BUBBLE BALLETS (SECOND BIT)

THE 'STUFF YOU NEED' BIT

Magic bubble mixture (see the first bit of the **BUBBLE BALLETS**)

Two yoghurt pots

Straws

Plasticine

THE 'WHAT TO DO WITH THE STUFF' BIT

Cut a hole in the side of both yoghurt pots and push a straw through each one. Put a bit of plasticine around the hole so that the air can't get out of the sides. Dip the rim of the yoghurt pots into the magic bubble mixture, blow a big

bubble (through the straws) in one, and a smaller bubble in the other. Hold the ends of the straws tight so that the bubbles stay up and then join the ends together. What happens to the bubbles? Does the little one get bigger or smaller?

Try the same thing again, but this time with a single straw. Cut a straw (like in **BUBBLE BALLETS – FIRST BIT**) at both ends and bend the bits back like flower petals. Make a small slit in the middle of the straw as well. Dip one end in the magic mixture and blow a small bubble through the middle slit. Then dip the other end in the magic mixture and keep blowing. You should end up with a big bubble at the one end and a smaller bubble at the other. Cover the slit with your finger so that the air is connected between the two bubbles and watch what happens. What does the small bubble do?

THE 'HEY BRILLIANT, IT WORKS' BIT

Watch what happens to the bubbles when you first join the straws together. If you start off with bubbles which are nearly the same size – does anything happen?

THE 'O.K., HOW DOES IT WORK?' BIT

For a bubble to exist at all, the air inside has to be at a greater pressure at first than the air outside – otherwise the air outside would squash it into nothing. The smaller a bubble is the more pressure there is inside it, so the small bubble is at a greater pressure than the bigger one. Now when you join the two bubbles the pressure difference pushes air from the smaller bubble through the straw to the bigger one so the small bubble gets even smaller and the big one gets even bigger.

ROLL UP, ROLL UP, SPIN THE BUCKET

THE 'STUFF YOU NEED' BIT

Seaside bucket, plastic putty or paint can, big yoghurt
pot or a wide plastic bottle

Water

Drinking straws

Blu-tack

THE 'WHAT TO DO WITH THE STUFF' BIT

We're going to make the bucket spin round just by using
water. Do it in the sink or the bath because it's very messy.
   First of all, empty your bucket and get someone to cut
four straw-sized holes near the bottom of the bucket, and
make each one a quarter of the way around from the next.
Seal up one end of each of the four straws by pushing
Blu-tack down it. Then, using a pin, make a small hole
about two centimetres from the same end. Fix each of the
straws into a hole in the bucket using glue or Blu-tack, and
make sure that the small hole in the straw is pointing
sideways – not down or up, but sideways. Tie a piece of
string to the handle of the seaside bucket and fill the bucket
with water. Hold it by the string, or tie it to something so it
can hang loosely, and the bucket will start to spin around as
the water shoots out of the holes in the straws. You're not
only going to be dirty and brilliant with this one, but very
wet too.

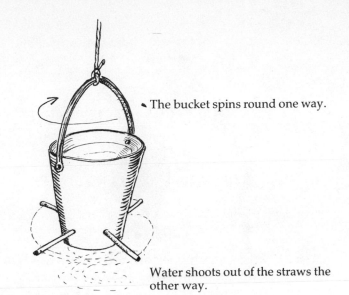

The bucket spins round one way.

Water shoots out of the straws the other way.

THE 'HEY BRILLIANT, IT WORKS' BIT

You can adjust it by using bigger straws, deeper buckets, bigger holes in the straws, or new designs based on the same thing. They are great fun hanging up in the bathroom.

THE 'O.K., HOW DOES IT WORK?' BIT

If you've done it right, the water will squirt out in spirals as the bucket spins round. If you stopped the bucket with your hand you would feel quite a force trying to keep it spinning. Three hundred years ago a great British scientist called Sir Isaac Newton found out that for every action, (that is a force going in one direction), there must be an equal and opposite reaction (the same amount of force but in the opposite direction).

Just like when a gun goes off, the person holding the gun feels a kick on their shoulder. The bullet has gone in one direction and so the gun must go in the other direction. Now, as the water (like the bullet) shoots out from the straws in a circular direction, so the bucket (like the gun) will want to spin the other way. Let go, and it will keep spinning as long as there is water in the bucket. When the bucket is full it will spin faster than when it is nearly empty. That's because the force of the water coming out of the straws will be greater, and so the force trying to spin the bucket will be greater as well.

MAKE AN UTTERLY BRILLIANT ROCKET

THE 'STUFF YOU NEED' BIT

A long sausage-shaped balloon

Drinking straw

Long piece of string – anything up to ten metres (thin
enough to thread through the straw)

Sellotape

THE 'WHAT TO DO WITH THE STUFF' BIT

Tie one end of the string to a door handle. Blow the balloon up and keep the end closed with one hand. (By the way, if you can use a balloon pump it makes this trick a lot easier.) Using Sellotape, stick the straw along the length of the balloon. Thread the string through the straw and stand with the balloon in one hand and the string as tight as possible in the other hand. Let go, stand back and the balloon shoots along the string. It is utterly brilliant.

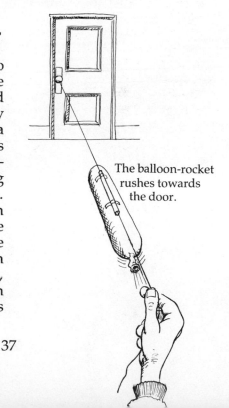

The balloon-rocket
rushes towards
the door.

37

THE 'HEY BRILLIANT, IT WORKS' BIT

Try blowing the balloon up only a little bit. Does the rocket go as far or as fast? Try using different shaped balloons. Does that make any difference to the rocket?

THE 'O.K., HOW DOES IT WORK?' BIT

Nearly three hundred years ago, Sir Isaac Newton discovered that for every action (a force going in one direction), there must be an equal and opposite reaction (another force going in the opposite direction). In this case, the air rushing out of the back of the balloon makes the balloon shoot forward down the string. The rocket you've just made is a very simple jet engine. In a jet engine, there is a special combustion chamber which is open at the back. When the fuel is burned, the very hot gases spurt out of the back and, just like with your balloon, the plane shoots forward.

TUMBLERS MAKE A STICKY BUSINESS

THE 'STUFF YOU NEED' BIT

Two plastic tumblers, with a smooth rim

Little bit of silver foil

Matches

Blotting paper

Water

THE 'WHAT TO DO WITH THE STUFF' BIT

WARNING: DON'T PLAY WITH MATCHES! GET A GROWN-UP TO HELP.

Cover the inside base of one of the tumblers with silver foil (it doesn't have to fit exactly, it's only there to stop the plastic from melting). Cut the blotting paper into squares which will cover the top of the tumbler with about three centimetres overlapping all round. Soak a square of blotting paper in water. Now, you've got to do this next bit really quickly. Strike a match and put it into the bottom of the tumbler, put the wet blotting paper on top, and then push the second tumbler (upside down) on top so that their rims are together. Hold it until the match goes out. If you've got a good seal the blotting paper will rip. Then lift the top tumbler and, hey presto, they've stuck together.

THE 'HEY BRILLIANT, IT WORKS' BIT

Try putting paperclips in the bottom tumbler, and do the experiment again. Does it make any difference? Remember that the blotting paper must be really wet, do the experiment quickly, and keep the rims smooth and pushed together.

THE 'O.K., HOW DOES IT WORK?' BIT

Once you've put the match in and made the seal, two things happen. First of all, the match burns up part of the air inside the tumblers. Flames need something called oxygen (which is part of air) to be able to burn. The match uses up all the oxygen inside the tumblers and then goes out. So now there is less *air* inside the tumblers, which means that there is less pressure. But there's still what we call 'atmospheric pressure' outside (see **DON'T BE STUPID – NEWSPAPERS CAN'T BREAK WOOD**). This atmospheric pressure is greater than the pressure inside the tumblers, and the difference between the two pushes the tumblers together.

You can do the same sort of thing with sink plungers. Put

40

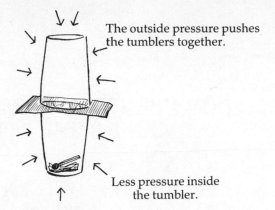

The outside pressure pushes the tumblers together.

Less pressure inside the tumbler.

two together, push out the air between them and it will take a really good heave to pull them apart.

Many years ago a man who lived in the German town of Magdeburg put two half spheres of metal together and sucked out the air inside. He wanted to show everybody in the town that he was right about atmospheric pressure, so he did it on a very grand scale. The metal spheres were really big and it took two teams of horses to pull them apart – to a great roar from the crowd, of course.

DON'T BE STUPID – NEWSPAPERS CAN'T BREAK WOOD

THE 'STUFF YOU NEED' BIT

Newspaper – the type with big pages is best

Thin bits of wood, say off a fruit crate

Hammer, cricket or rounders bat, or a block of wood

THE 'WHAT TO DO WITH THE STUFF' BIT

It's true – you *can* use newspaper to break wood.

Get a thin piece of wood, like a slat from a fruit crate (just ask the local supermarket or greengrocer), and put it on to a bench with about fifteen centimetres sticking out over the end. Now, if you hit it with a cricket bat, it will go right up into the air and probably break a lightbulb. So, we need something to hold it down. This is where the newspaper comes in. Fold a couple of sheets of newspaper into quar-

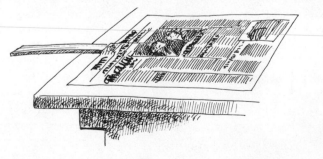

ters and lay them over the wood, hit the end of the wood and the wood will still go up in the air but not as much. Open the sheets out into a half and try again: the same thing will happen but the wood won't go as far. Open the newspaper right out and smooth it over the wood. Now give the wood an almighty whack and the wood should break in two. So, you've used newspaper to break wood.

THE 'HEY BRILLIANT, IT WORKS' BIT

Try using different sizes of newspaper and lengths of wood. Really give the wood a good hit though, otherwise it might not work properly.

THE 'O.K., HOW DOES IT WORK?' BIT

The newspaper has what is known as atmospheric pressure pushing down on it. Imagine that above you there are about three miles of air in what we call the earth's atmosphere. Now, although air is light compared to metal, it still weighs something and if there is a lot of it pushing down, like in the atmosphere, the 'pressure' amounts to quite a lot. If you imagine a column of air pushing down on to something from above, then obviously the bigger the area (say a table compared to a pencil), the bigger the column of air above it and the bigger the force acting on it. As you unfold the newspaper you are making its area much bigger, so the force acting on it will be much bigger as well. In fact, the air above the newspaper weighs about five tons, so when you whack the wood the paper doesn't budge. Well, that's not exactly true because the paper does lift up slightly when the wood breaks, but it's sucked back down again very quickly. That's because as the wood breaks, the newspaper tries to go up in the air. But if you've done a really good job of smoothing out the paper, then air can't get into

the space. A vacuum (a sort of sucking space) is created underneath the paper which pulls it back down on to the table. Hey presto! The trick works brilliantly – well, it should anyway . . .!

WE ALL LIVE IN A PLASTIC SUBMARINE

THE 'STUFF YOU NEED' BIT

Plastic bottle (about a litre)

Plastic straw

Blu-tack

Water

THE 'WHAT TO DO WITH THE STUFF' BIT

Firstly, empty the lemonade out of the bottle . . . Now, refill the bottle with water so that it's overflowing. Lower a five centimetre long straw into a bowl of cold water so that half of it is under water. Still holding it under water, plug the top with some Blu-tack. Then put your finger over the open end and bring it out of the water. Turn it upside down and stick a small, snake-like bit of Blu-tack around the outside of the open end.

Are you with it so far? Good.

Now put the straw back into the bowl of water (open end down), without losing the water inside it and make it just float (nearly sink), by altering the amount of Blu-tack at the bottom. Once it just floats, transfer the straw (the diver) to the bottle of water, making sure that you don't lose the water inside it. Check that the bottle is full of water and put the top on. It sounds like there's a lot to do but there isn't really, it's just a bit fiddly. Squeeze the bottle and the diver will sink. When you let go of the bottle, the diver will rise. Just like a submarine!

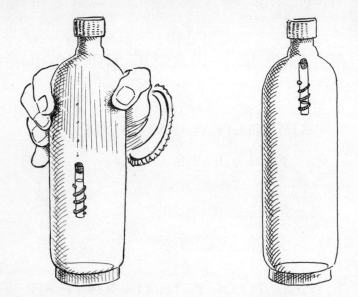

When the bottle is squeezed the water level in the straw rises.

When the bottle is released the water level in the straw falls.

THE 'HEY BRILLIANT, IT WORKS' BIT

The key things to remember are that the Blu-tack plug at the top has to be on tight, and the bottle must be full to the brim. Also, the diver must only just float near the surface of the bowl. When you've got it right you can make a monster or a submarine, maybe out of a plastic bag and stick it on to the front of the diver to make it look really good.

THE 'O.K., HOW DOES IT WORK?' BIT

Watch the straw carefully and see what happens to the water level inside it. When the straw just floats in the bottle, the water level is quite low in the straw. It's quite easy to squeeze air into a smaller space, it isn't so easy to squeeze water. So when you squeeze the bottle, the water forces the air into a smaller space making the straw heavier, and so it sinks. When you let go of the bottle the air is let out again, the straw gets lighter and it rises.

A submarine dives by letting water into special tanks: that makes it heavier, and it sinks. When it wants to come to the surface again, it blows air (which it carries in compressed air containers) into the tanks: the water escapes, the submarine gets lighter, and it rises to the top.

HOW HIGH IS A WATERFALL?

THE 'STUFF YOU NEED' BIT

Washing-up liquid bottle or plastic bottle

Water

THE 'WHAT TO DO WITH THE STUFF' BIT

Get the tallest plastic bottle you can find and make three holes in it, one at the top, one in the middle, and one very near to the bottom. Fill it with water (that's the messy bit, so be near the sink) and watch what happens to the waterfalls.

The one at the top is the weakest and the one at the bottom
is the strongest, really spurting out.

THE 'HEY BRILLIANT, IT WORKS' BIT

If you make the holes quite small, then the effect is really
clear. If you're feeling messy then do it with an old piece of
drainpipe: you can soak everybody then, not just yourself.

THE 'O.K., HOW DOES IT WORK?' BIT

Imagine that you are a drop of water inside the bottle. Then
if you are near the top, there will only be a little bit of water
pushing down on top of you. The closer you get to the
bottom though, the deeper the water gets, and the more
'pressure' you feel (there's more water pushing down). So,
at the top, the 'pressure' is quite low and the water trickles
out of the bottle. At the bottom, the 'pressure' is much
greater and the water bursts out through the hole.

It's exactly the same with water in the house. If your tank
of water is on the first floor, then your shower won't be very
strong, but the higher up you can get the tank of water (into
the loft, say), the more 'pressure' there will be, and the
stronger the force of water coming out of the tap or the
shower.

STICKY STRING

THE 'STUFF YOU NEED' BIT

Ice cubes

Thick piece of string

Salt

THE 'WHAT TO DO WITH THE STUFF' BIT

Put an ice cube on a plate or a bowl or something. Soak one end of the string in water and then lay it on top of the ice cube. Sprinkle a mound of salt all along the string. Wait ten seconds and then lift the string: the ice cube will come up as well. What a brilliant magician you are!

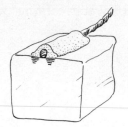

THE 'HEY BRILLIANT, IT WORKS' BIT

Try using a matchstick instead of the string. See what happens if you don't soak the string. Is it easier or more difficult?

THE 'O.K., HOW DOES IT WORK?' BIT

In the winter when it snows, the roads are sprayed with grit or salt to melt the ice. Ice is just frozen water, and it freezes at a certain temperature called 'zero degrees Celsius' or 0°C. When you sprinkle salt on to the ice it mixes up with the thin layer of water on top of the ice, and that mixture is called a 'salt solution'. Now, it needs to be much colder than 'zero degrees Celsius' to freeze this salt solution, so as long as it isn't too cold the salt solution stays as a slushy mess and doesn't freeze over. That's why it is much safer to drive on salted or gritted roads in winter.

When you lay the wet string on to the ice cube and then sprinkle the salt on top, the ice directly underneath the salt (but not under the string) melts to form a salt solution. To be able to do this, it has to steal some heat from somewhere, and it steals the heat from the water in the string. The water in the string gets colder and freezes over. It freezes over so much that the string gets stuck onto the ice cube. So when you lift it, the ice cube comes up as well.

MAKE AN UTTERLY BRILLIANT RECORD

THE 'STUFF YOU NEED' BIT

Record – twelve inch

Piece of string

Piece of card

THE 'WHAT TO DO WITH THE STUFF' BIT

Cut a hole out of a small piece of card so that it fits over the hole in your record. Thread a piece of string about sixty centimetres long through the record and the card and tie a big knot underneath to keep it in place. Hold the top end of

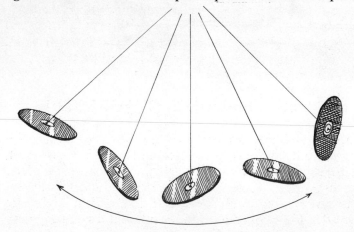

the string and swing the record from side to side. Nothing special happens, it just flops about.

Now spin the record really fast, and swing it from side to side again. The record doesn't flop around this time; it stays horizontal while it spins, no matter how hard you swing it. You've made an utterly brilliant record.

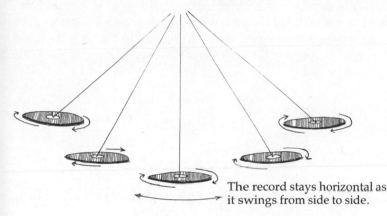

The record stays horizontal as it swings from side to side.

THE 'HEY BRILLIANT, IT WORKS' BIT

Roll a bicycle wheel and it will stay upright while it's rolling, but once it stops it falls over. If you're feeling really adventurous put two handles in the middle of a bicycle wheel, one either side. Hold it away from you and get someone to spin it round. Now try to tilt it over – it won't go, will it? All these things happen for the same reason. READ ON.

THE 'O.K., HOW DOES IT WORK?' BIT

Anything which is spinning or rolling has something very special about it – it doesn't want to change the way in which it's spinning. When an object is spinning in a certain plane (at a certain tilt), it doesn't want to change that tilt, and you have to give it a big push to make it do so. That's why the bicycle wheel is so hard to tilt over when it's spinning fast. So if you start the record spinning in a horizontal plane (that's level to the ground), it will carry on spinning horizontally even though you're rocking it from side to side. The record is acting like a 'gyroscope'.

Gyroscopes are used to keep planes and rockets and ships steady by acting artificial horizons. Once they are set spinning they stay in the same plane all the time and so no matter how much the ship rocks on the sea the gyroscope, like the record, will always stay in the same plane. Very often, these gyroscopes send messages to the engines and things in ships to tell them how to keep as level as possible on a rough sea.

LOOPY LEVERS

THE 'STUFF YOU NEED' BIT

Ruler and three ten-pence pieces

Pencil

Matchbox

Bit of plasticine

THE 'WHAT TO DO WITH THE STUFF' BIT

Plonk a small block of plasticine on top of the matchbox, and push the pencil in, sideways down. Then balance the ruler on the top. Put a single coin at one end of the ruler and two coins on the other side of the ruler, adjusting them until they balance. Note how far away from the balancing point

(the pencil) the coins are. The single coin should be twice as far away as the two coins. Try it again with three coins at one end and make a note of the distances.

Now, levers can be used to lift all sorts of things. Try to lift a heavy book using your ruler as a lever. Balance the ruler near its middle point, put the book at one end and push down on the other end. Does the book lift up easily? No? Well, push the pencil (the balancing point of the ruler) nearer to the book. Push down on the other end again – can you lift it now? Keep moving the pencil so that it gets closer to the book. Eventually you will lift the book.

With the pencil in the same place (that is, not in the middle), take the book off and put a coin on the end instead. Drop a coin on to the other end (which should be sticking up in the air) and the coin on the farside will do a somersault.

THE 'HEY BRILLIANT, IT WORKS' BIT

Try lifting all sorts of things. Measure the weights of what you're lifting and keep changing the position of the ruler until you start to see what is happening. Flick tiddlywinks – does that remind you of a lever?

THE 'O.K., HOW DOES IT WORK?' BIT

Levers allow you to lift heavy weights using just a small pushing force. Levers lift things most easily when the weight to lift is nearest to the 'fulcrum' (the balancing point) and the pushing force (your hand or the coin) is as far away from the 'fulcrum' as possible. In this way, it's possible to prise things open using crow-bars or open a tin lid with a coin – another lever.

Acrobats use levers in their tricks. The acrobat who is thrown into the air stands as close to the 'fulcrum' as possible, and his partner jumps on to the see-saw as far

away from the 'fulcrum' as possible. In that way, he gives
the somersaulting acrobat the maximum push into the air
and the two of them give a brilliant show.

BET YOU CAN'T HOLD A CUP WITH ONE FINGER

THE 'STUFF YOU NEED' BIT

Plasticine

Piece of wire (coat hanger, or something)

Potato, plastic cup, pencil, knives, forks, paper, and bits and pieces

THE 'WHAT TO DO WITH THE STUFF' BIT

Get the cup, and stuff either a cork or a lump of plasticine through the handle. Stick two knives or forks through the

cork so that they hang down underneath the cup. Put the cup on your finger and adjust it so that it balances. The heavier the knives and the lighter the cup the better.

Stick bits of wood, matchsticks or something into your potato to make a potato man. Then stick one end of a curved piece of wire into the potato (near the bottom) and the other end into a big lump of plasticine. Stand the potato man on a table edge – the plasticine will make it balance.

Try making a tightrope walker of your potato man by standing him on a tight piece of string and see what happens.

THE 'HEY BRILLIANT, IT WORKS' BIT

Really have a good go at using all sorts of things. What you're trying to do is get the most weight underneath the balancing point, which may be your finger, the string, or the potato man's feet. Go mad and use everything in the house. Balance eggs and make your Mum or Dad turn blue.

THE 'O.K., HOW DOES IT WORK?' BIT

You can make anything balance if you can get its centre of gravity directly below its balancing point. The centre of gravity is the middle of a body's weight. So by using heavy things like knives and forks and plasticine we can alter the centre of gravity of the cup bringing it below the balancing point.

IF YOU WANT TO BE LOUD, THEN MAKE A MEGAPHONE

THE 'STUFF YOU NEED' BIT

Big piece of card

Glue

Plastic funnels

Piece of tube

A friend

THE 'WHAT TO DO WITH THE STUFF' BIT

Cut the card into a really big circle and then cut a little circle out of the middle. Make it into a cone with a hole at the peak for you to shout down. Glue it all together. This is where you need a friend. Go outside and, speaking quietly, keep repeating the word 'brilliant'. Your friend must keep walk-

61

ing away from you slowly (but facing you all the time) and then he must tell you when he can't hear you any more. Make a mark in the grass or on the pavement. Next use the megaphone and do the same thing again, still speaking quietly. See how much further he can go. Mark it again and see the difference.

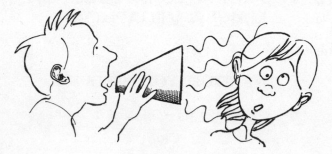

THE 'HEY BRILLIANT, IT WORKS' BIT

Try changing the size of the megaphone and see if your friend can go any further away.

THE 'O.K., HOW DOES IT WORK?' BIT

Sound is just vibrating air which has a special effect on your ears. Your ears then pass messages on to the brain to say

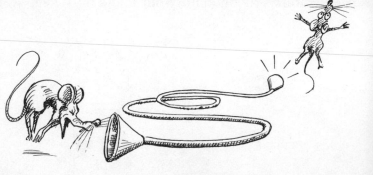

that you're 'hearing' something. Now, the more the air vibrates, the louder the sound. When you speak normally, your mouth is making the air vibrate in a certain way, but when you shout, the air vibrates even more. This increase in vibration makes the sound much louder.

When you speak through a megaphone, the whole card starts to vibrate which in turn vibrates more air (because it has a large surface) and the sound becomes louder. That's why your friend can go further away from you when you use the megaphone.

SPEAKING CUPS

THE 'STUFF YOU NEED' BIT

Two yoghurt pots

A really long ball of string

A friend

THE 'WHAT TO DO WITH THE STUFF' BIT

Make a small hole in the bottom of each pot. Push the ends
of the string through each pot and tie a knot at each end.
You can make the string as long as you like – up to as much
as twenty metres long. Now you need to make sure of
two things before you talk to each other. The first thing is
that the string has to be pulled really tight. The second
thing is that the string mustn't touch anything. Now one
of you whisper into a pot and the other one listen. Hey
presto – a brilliant telephone system.

THE 'HEY BRILLIANT, IT WORKS' BIT

See what happens if the string touches something – a wall
or fence. Does it work any better, or is it worse? Try
slackening the string – what happens now? Try using two
different sized and shaped pots, does it still work?

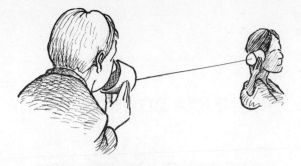

THE 'O.K., HOW DOES IT WORK?' BIT

Sound is just vibrating air which, when it reaches our ears, turns magically into what we know as sound. Sound has to be transmitted through something, maybe through air or water or along a piece of string. In space, however, there isn't any air and if two astronauts tried to speak to each other normally – they couldn't. If there isn't any air then the sound can't be transmitted.

When the string is tight and you speak into one of the pots, you are making the pot vibrate. The pot passes on the vibration (transmits the sound) through the string to the other pot. When that pot picks up the vibration, the air at that end starts to vibrate in exactly the same way and so your friend can hear you speaking and whispering. In this way, the sound isn't transmitted through air, but along the piece of string.

SOUNDS A BIT DUFF TO ME

THE 'STUFF YOU NEED' BIT

Two cardboard tubes

Couple of books

Clock or radio

Bits of stuff to test – like cork, cardboard, plates, tin

THE 'WHAT TO DO WITH THE STUFF' BIT

Sound waves are funny things. They bounce off some
things and don't bounce off others. When you drop a stone
on to a table, it makes a noise; drop it on to the carpet and i
doesn't make as much noise. To test how good or bac
different materials are at reflecting sound do the next trick

Put a cardboard tube on top of a couple of books and pu
one end close to the clock or radio. Put the other end near tc
a plate (you'll probably have to make the plate stand up
somehow or other). Hold the second tube close to the plate
(make sure that the two tubes are over five centimetres
apart) and listen through the other end. How well can you
hear the clock or radio? The sound of the clock is coming
through the first tube, bouncing off the plate, and travelling
through the second tube straight into your ear. What is the
sound like, is it loud, tinny or soft? Try pieces of cork
instead of the plate, or a block of wood, books, cottonwoo
or metal. What happens to the sound?

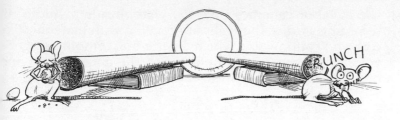

THE 'HEY BRILLIANT IT WORKS' BIT

The results should all be different. The smooth surfaces like the plate will bounce the sound back, and soft materials like cottonwool will deaden it.

THE 'O.K., HOW DOES IT WORK?' BIT

Well, the shiny materials bounce the sound back. The soft materials like cottonwool and cork absorb the sound by changing the vibration (which is what sound is) into heat inside the material.

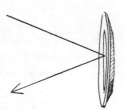

Most of the sound is reflected by the plate.

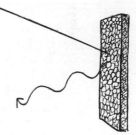

Most of the sound is absorbed by the cork.

Sound engineers use various materials to produce different sounds in offices, recording studios and concert halls. Most of the time they are trying to get rid of echoes which could lead to poor sound quality: for that reason they don't use metal or ceramics (like the plate) inside a studio. In recording studios the walls are covered with materials like cork and cottonwool, which ensure that only the singer's voice or the musician's notes reach the microphone, and not stray sounds or echoes.

SINGING BOTTLES

THE 'STUFF YOU NEED' BIT

Two identical glass bottles

Water

A friend

THE 'WHAT TO DO WITH THE STUFF' BIT

Hold one of the bottles close to your ear and get your friend
(who should be about ninety centimetres away) to blow
across the top of another bottle so that a note sings out. You
should hear exactly the same note coming out of your
bottle.

69

Now fill one of the bottles with a little bit of water and do the same trick. Can you still hear the note echoing in your bottle? Probably not. Now you hear it – now you don't.

THE 'HEY BRILLIANT, IT WORKS' BIT

Try using different shaped bottles and see if it still works. You'll find that the bottles have to be exactly the same.

THE 'O.K., HOW DOES IT WORK?' BIT

Everything in the world – you, me, a bit of wood, a glass, the cooker, a bottle – absolutely everything in the world is vibrating. Most of the time we don't notice that something is vibrating because the movements are very, very small. Some things vibrate very slowly and some things vibrate quickly, but everything in the world vibrates at its own frequency (speed).

Now, because the two bottles are identical, they vibrate at exactly the same frequency. When your friend blows over the bottle he vibrates the air inside. This vibration is passed through the air in the room to your bottle. Because your bottle is identical, the same note is produced and what's known as 'resonance' occurs. Resonance is a big vibration which occurs when the natural frequency of the object (in this case, the bottle) is the same as an applied frequency (in this case, the vibration of the air). When you add water you change the natural frequency of the bottle, resonance doesn't occur this time and you don't hear a thing.

When you tune your radio you change its natural frequency until it hits the same frequency as the radio waves. When that happens, and you tune into your favourite station, resonance happens and you hear the music coming out of the radio.

EXCUSE ME, SIR, IS THAT EGG RAW OR BOILED?

THE 'STUFF YOU NEED' BIT

One raw egg

One hard-boiled egg

THE 'WHAT TO DO WITH THE STUFF' BIT

If Mum keeps boiled eggs as well as fresh ones in the fridge, you can have a great game swapping them round and then making her guess which one is which.

Get hold of one of the eggs and spin it round. If it spins quickly, it's the hard-boiled egg. Now stop it with your finger, and it will stop stone dead. Give the other egg a good spin. If it only wobbles around, it is definitely the raw egg. Stop it and then let it go quickly, it will start to wobble again.

The hard-boiled egg spins.

The raw egg wobbles.

THE 'HEY BRILLIANT, IT WORKS' BIT

What else wobbles around, and what else spins very quickly? Try oranges or apples, then try some sloppy things in containers and see what happens.

THE 'O.K., HOW DOES IT WORK?' BIT

The hard-boiled egg is solid and spins just like a ball or a stone. When you stop it, it stops completely.

However there are different layers of egg white and yolk inside the raw egg which gurgle around lazily. When you spin it, these layers juggle round making the egg wobble unevenly. When you stop it, you've only stopped the shell but the yolk and the white are still moving around. So, when you take your finger off, the shell picks up the movement of the insides and starts to wobble again. If you've tried any other things, you may have noticed that solid objects spin round well, but anything that has liquid inside it, wobbles round sloppily.

THAT NEEDLE IS A COMPASS, SIR

THE 'STUFF YOU NEED' BIT

A bar magnet, a darning needle

Piece of cork in a saucer of water

A compass (not essential)

THE 'WHAT TO DO WITH THE STUFF' BIT

It's dead easy to make lots of magnets out of one magnet. Get a darning needle (that's one which is quite long and thick), and hold it down on a flat surface. Stroke the needle about fifty times with one end of your magnet, making sure that you always stroke it in the same direction. Lift the magnet when you reach the end and go back to the beginning to make a sort of circular movement. The needle is now a magnet. Test it by seeing if it can pick up light bits of metal.

O.K., so the needle's a magnet. Now, balance the needle on a piece of cork which is floating in the saucer of water. The needle comes to rest facing North-South. If you've done this at home, then you'll know whereabouts South is. South is the direction from where the sun always shines at noon. Check it out with an ordinary compass. Stick a piece of paper underneath the saucer and mark where North and South is, and there is your brand new compass.

THE 'HEY BRILLIANT, IT WORKS' BIT

Try bringing one end of the bar magnet to the needle, and then the other and see what happens. One end will attract the needle and the other will repel it (push it away).

THE 'O.K., HOW DOES IT WORK?' BIT

Throughout history, armies and travellers have used magnets to find direction. About six hundred years ago, sailors would use the stars to travel, but when the skies were cloudy and they could not see the stars they were lost. The compass was brilliant for them because now they could 'see by night'. Soon they started to travel to new continents, across oceans, without fear of being lost.

Your needle becomes a magnet because iron and steel

(like your needle) are special materials which are made up of tiny little magnets inside. Normally, these tiny magnets are jumbled up in different directions and cancel each other out, but when you stroke a bar magnet along the needle, they line up to face in the same direction. Your needle becomes a magnet with a North and a South pole. When it spins in the water, it's just lining up with the North and South magnetic poles of the Earth, which gives you a brilliant homemade compass. The only problem is that it's not easy to carry round in a saucer of water. . . .

HOW CAN A LEMON LIGHT MY TORCH?

THE 'STUFF YOU NEED' BIT

Jam jar, a coin, a torch bulb in a holder

Lemons

An old battery – the type you use in a torch or a toy

Malt vinegar

Two lengths of copper wire

THE 'WHAT TO DO WITH THE STUFF' BIT

There are two different ways to make a battery using old bits and pieces. First of all though, attach the two lengths of copper wire to either end of the torch bulb holder. Secondly, take the old battery to pieces. You'll have to cut off the outer metal casing, which is made of a silvery coloured metal called zinc. Then, pull out the rod which is in the middle (this is made of carbon and is black). Wash both bits and bend the zinc into a coin sized square.

For the first battery, wrap one length of the copper wire around the zinc casing, then wrap the other wire around a coppery coloured coin (say a two-pence piece). Lower both of them into the empty jam jar, but make sure that they don't touch. Pour in the vinegar and you should see the lamp light up.

For the second battery, make two cuts in a lemon and push the zinc (which is attached to the copper wire) in one cut, and the carbon rod (which should be attached to the other wire) in the other cut. The bulb should light up again.

THE 'HEY BRILLIANT, IT WORKS' BIT

If the lemons prove a bit difficult, try making a couple of 'lemon batteries' and joining them up using more copper wire. Check that all the connections are right. In the first battery, try different things instead of the coin: maybe a metal washer, a piece of aluminium foil, the carbon rod from the battery or a ten pence piece. You should also try using different things instead of the vinegar: maybe lemon juice or salty water. When does the lamp burn brightest of all?

THE 'O.K., HOW DOES IT WORK?' BIT

It's a fact of life that metals can do certain things that other bits and pieces like pottery and carpets can't. One of the things that metals can do is produce electricity, and whenever you put two different metals together separated by what's known as a conducting liquid (something that can carry electricity) you will get electricity. Now that's true whatever type of metals you use, and whatever type of conducting liquid you use. The clever thing is to use two metals which will give you the most electricity, together with the best type of conducting liquid. That's what you've been doing when you change the coin for other types of metals; and if you haven't been doing that, then do it now.

MAKE AN UTTERLY AND COMPLETELY BRILLIANT NERVE TESTER

THE 'STUFF YOU NEED' BIT

A three volt battery

Wire coat hanger

A couple of lengths of copper wire

Torch bulb in its holder

Plasticine and pliers

THE 'WHAT TO DO WITH THE STUFF' BIT

This machine is the type of thing you see at funfairs. You try to run a loop of wire along a bendy track without touching it. If you get it wrong a buzzer goes off. Our nerve tester uses a lightbulb instead of a buzzer just because they're easier to get hold of, but if you've got an old electric buzzer use it – you'll be very loud and very brilliant.

First of all, cut a long piece of thick wire from the coat hanger and bend it up and down, keeping the ends fairly straight: this is going to be your nerve testing track. Next, connect one end of the nerve tester to the battery with a piece of copper wire.

With another piece of wire, make a loop which is big enough to fit easily around your nerve tester: it'll look like a bubble blower when you've finished. The smaller you make the circle the more difficult the test will be. Put a bit of tape around the handle to make it more comfortable to hold. Connect this piece of wire to your bulb, and then the bulb to the battery. Loop the bubble blower on to the nerve tester and stick the tester into two lumps of plasticine to keep it upright and steady. Now when the bubble blower touches the nerve tester, the light should come on. So start with the bubble blower at one end and see how many times the light comes on before you get to the end. See if you can get to the end without the light coming on. Pilots often try games like this to see how good their senses are.

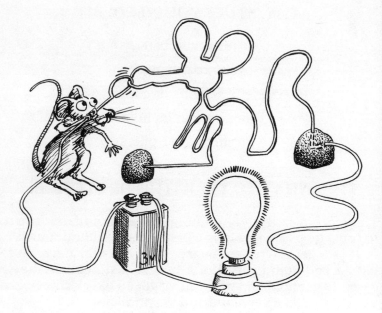

THE 'HEY BRILLIANT, IT WORKS' BIT

If you find it too hard, then make the bubble blower a bit larger or the nerve tester less bendy. Try it with a buzzer. Just detach it from the battery when you go to bed, and it'll be ready again next time you want a go on it.

THE 'O.K., HOW DOES IT WORK?' BIT

When the bubble blower touches the wire, electricity is allowed to flow around a circuit. The circuit goes from the battery, through the bulb and the bubble blower, then through the nerve tester and finally back to the battery. If there is a gap anywhere in the circuit (when the bubble blower doesn't touch the nerve tester) electricity can't flow and the light stays off. When the bubble blower touches the nerve tester, the circuit is completed and the light or the buzzer comes on again.

STRANGE HAPPENINGS WITH A PLASTIC COMB

THE 'STUFF YOU NEED' BIT

Woollen cloth (maybe a cleaning cloth, or a woolly scarf)

Plastic comb

Piece of newspaper

Coin, jar, match

Ping pong ball

THE 'WHAT TO DO WITH THE STUFF' BIT

If you've got all that stuff, then you can do a whole pile of tricks. Take the comb first of all, and rub it up and down lots of times with a woollen cloth. Run the tap in the kitchen or in the bath so that there is a thin trickle of water coming out. Now bring the comb up to the water, but don't let it get wet. The water will bend towards the comb, just like magic.

Another one to do is to rub the comb with the cloth again and bring it up to the ping pong ball. The ball will come towards it. Move the comb around slowly and the ball will follow.

If you rub the comb again, try picking up little pieces of things like tissue paper, feathers, and bits of fluff.

Hold a sheet of newspaper up against a wall. Rub it hard with a ruler all over and then take your hands away. The newspaper should stay where it is. You can do the same sort of trick with a balloon. Rub it up and down against your tummy (with clothes on, please!) and let go. The balloon will stay up and not fall to the floor.

This is a brilliant trick. Get a coin, say a ten-pence piece,

and balance it upright on a table. Balance a match on top of it and put a glass over the top to cover them both. Then bet someone that they can't make the match fall over without touching the glass or the table. To do it, rub your comb with the cloth and wave it around close to the glass. The match will fall off, and you win the bet.

THE 'HEY BRILLIANT, IT WORKS' BIT

There are loads of tricks you can do like this. The key thing is to always make sure that the stuff is dry and then it will work really well. Try rubbing different materials together like wool, glass, silk, acrylic, rubber, cotton and see what happens and which works best of all.

THE 'O.K., HOW DOES IT WORK?' BIT

All the tricks you've done work because of what we call 'static electricity'. Sometimes, when you take your clothes off at night you might get tiny electric shocks and see sparks. That's because of static electricity which is produced whenever you rub two different materials together. Some materials produce more static than others and plastic, nylon and wool are probably some of the best at the job. The way to get rid of static is with moisture – water or damp breath. When something like the comb is 'charged up' with static electricity, then it will attract uncharged things like water or bits of paper towards it.

MAKE AN UTTERLY BRILLIANT HOVERCRAFT

THE 'STUFF YOU NEED' BIT

Balloon

Margarine tub with a flat bottom

Cotton reel

Glue

THE 'WHAT TO DO WITH THE STUFF' BIT

Make a small hole in the centre of the margarine tub. Then, glue the cotton reel so that the middle of it goes over the hole. Let it dry well otherwise the cotton reel comes off. Now try to flick the tub across a smooth topped table. It doesn't go very far, does it? How can we make it go further?

Well, blow up the balloon and put the end over the cotton reel. Air starts to shoot out of the bottom and lifts the tub off the table. Just by flicking it across a smooth table top, you can make it go really fast.

THE 'HEY BRILLIANT, IT WORKS' BIT

If the air isn't coming out quickly enough, try making the hole a little bigger. What happens when the balloon goes flat, does the tub still move quickly? Try using different shaped balloons and see if it changes anything. You can even have hovercraft races.

THE 'O.K., HOW DOES IT WORK?' BIT

When you flick the tub across the table top without the help of the balloon, it stops. Friction between the tub and the table has slowed it down. But when you use the balloon, it blows out a layer of air underneath the tub. Now, there is only friction between the air and the tub. This friction is really small so when you flick the tub this time it moves very easily.

A hovercraft works just like the tub: it blows air underneath it – not from a balloon but from a big fan inside the engine. The air makes the hovercraft lift up so that it only needs a little push to get it moving. Boats and ships can only work on the sea, they are completely useless on the ground, but hovercrafts are better than ships in that way because they can work on both.

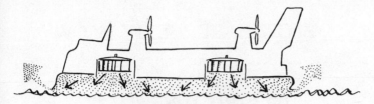

Air is blown downwards.

BLOW HARD, BETTY, BLOW

THE 'STUFF YOU NEED' BIT

Hairdryer

Ping pong balls, apples, string

Piece of paper

THE 'WHAT TO DO WITH THE STUFF' BIT

There are a load of things you can do with a hairdryer other than just dry your hair. Interested? Then try these.

Turn the hairdryer on, and hold it so that the air is going straight up to the sky. Put a ping pong ball on top of the dryer and it looks as though it's kept in mid air by magic. If you tilt the hairdryer to one side, the ball will stay there and then suddenly, if you tilt it too far, it will fall to the ground.

Try hanging two apples by a piece of string and hold them so that they are about two centimetres apart. Blow air in between them, and see what happens. You would probably expect the apples to blow apart but they don't – they come together.

Bend a piece of paper not quite in half (the stiffer the paper is the better), and glue the two ends together so that the upper edge is curved and the lower edge is flat. Put a pencil through the gap to make the paper hang down. Blow air just over the top of the paper and it will rise up like an aeroplane wing.

THE 'HEY BRILLIANT, IT WORKS' BIT

See what else you can use instead of the apples. Can the hairdryer keep a tennis ball in the air? Try using the hairdryer at different speed settings and see what happens.

THE 'O.K., HOW DOES IT WORK?' BIT

It's dead simple this one. Anything like an airstream or even a stream of water has less pressure inside it when it's moving than when it's still, and the faster it moves the less the pressure becomes. The air between the apples has less pressure than normal when you turn the hairdryer on, but there is still normal air pressure outside the apples. The difference between the two pushes the apples together.

If the ping pong ball tries to go out of the airstream it's pushed back. The pressure outside the fast stream of air is greater than inside and this difference in pressure keeps pushing the ball back, keeping it above the hairdryer.

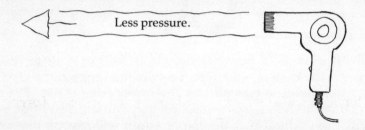

Less pressure.

When you blow air over the piece of paper, there is less pressure *above* it than *below* and again the difference in pressure pushes the paper up. An aeroplane flies in exactly the same way. As it rushes along the runway the pressure below the wing becomes greater than the pressure above it and the massive difference is enough to lift even a jumbo jet into the sky.

PRINT A DIRTY, LOUD AND BRILLIANT T-SHIRT

THE 'STUFF YOU NEED' BIT

Photocopy of whatever you want to print (see special note about printing words)

Plain T-shirt

Bottle of turps or white spirit

Water and a bit of washing-up liquid

Small paintbrush and a wallpaper roller (not a furry paint roller)

Warm metal tray

THE 'WHAT TO DO WITH THE STUFF' BIT

I'm going to tell you the best way to do this first of all, but you can print without all the stuff I'm going to tell you about.

Mix together about a cup of water with half a cup of white spirit and a squeeze of washing-up liquid. You should end up with a milky mixture when it's shaken. Brush the photocopy with lots of the mixture first on the back and then on the front. If you've got one, warm up a metal tray (you can use a cool iron to do this), and put it inside the T-shirt under where you want the picture to go. Put the wet photocopy face down on to the T-shirt and roll really hard all over the paper with the wallpaper roller so that a lot of the ink comes out. You can use the back of a spoon if you haven't got a roller. Try not to move the photocopy while you're doing this, otherwise it will smudge. Peel the photocopy off and, hey presto!, the picture will be on the T-shirt. It should be waterproof but to make sure spray it with waterproofing spray which you can buy from an art shop.

THE 'HEY BRILLIANT, IT WORKS' BIT

Make sure that you practise on old bits of cloth first and get lots of photocopies of the picture because you'll need a new one every time you print.

If you want to print words, then tell the person in the photocopying shop that you need a transparency (acetate sheet) of the words and a 'reverse' copy of your design, and they'll sort you out. You can even do your own designs as long as you get them photocopied. For the best results try to get fresh photocopies as the ink on them will still be reasonably new. Try printing on other things like pieces of wood and you'll get some cracking results.

THE 'O.K., HOW DOES IT WORK?' BIT

White spirit is often used as paint stripper and when you put the mixture on to the photocopy it soaks in and tries to lift the ink off the paper. When you roll the wet photocopy against the T-shirt material the ink lifts off the paper and passes on to the T-shirt instead. If you've done a good job, then your print will be good too.

HOW CAN RED CABBAGE BE BLUE?

THE 'STUFF YOU NEED' BIT

Boiled red cabbage, and a couple of glasses

Vinegar, bicarbonate of soda (baking soda)

Washing soda, tea, toothpaste and loads of other stuff

THE 'WHAT TO DO WITH THE STUFF' BIT

Slice up a few leaves of red cabbage, put them in a saucepan, cover them with water and boil them for five minutes. Leave the pan to cool, strain the cabbage and keep the purple water.

Pour a little bit of the cabbage water into a couple of glasses. Add a dollop of vinegar to one of the glasses and a teaspoon of bicarbonate of soda to the other. The purple cabbage water turns blue immediately in the bicarbonate of soda glass, and pink in the vinegar glass.

Try putting some vinegar into the bicarbonate of soda glass and the mixture will turn back to purple.

Try other things in a new batch of cabbage water. What happens with washing soda, tea, toothpaste, lemon juice, orange squash, salt. What colour does the water turn?

THE 'HEY BRILLIANT, IT WORKS' BIT

By now, you'll see that all of the things you've tried fall into one of three groups: one turns the water pink; one turns the water blue and the last group has no effect on the colour whatsoever. The names of these groups are acids (turn it pink), bases or alkalis (turn it blue), and the neutral group which has no effect whatsoever. The cabbage water is called the 'indicator' because it points out which group each test falls into. Obviously you can't keep boiling cabbage forever, so a cheap and easy way to do these tests is to bomb along to a chemist and ask for some litmus paper: this is just paper which has had an 'indicator' soaked into it already. Litmus paper tells you a lot more about acids and bases. Dip a strip of it into your test and it will tell you exactly how acidic or how strong a base something is.

Try testing some rain and see how acidic that is, the more acidic it is the more damage it will do to plants and buildings.

THE 'O.K., HOW DOES IT WORK?' BIT

Acids and alkalis have different effects on all sorts of things, but when they are used together one tends to cancel out the effect of the other. When you add vinegar to the already

blue cabbage water, it turns back to the original purple colour: this is called 'neutralising' (killing it off). A bee sting is very acidic and so to take away some of the pain (to neutralise it) take the sting out and rub in some bicarbonate of soda (a base) or a special cream which contains a base. Wasp stings are exactly the opposite, they contain bases and have to be treated with an acidic substance to neutralise the effect.

CARNATIONS, CELERY AND RAINBOWS

THE 'STUFF YOU NEED' BIT

Carnations, celery and a rainbow – not really

Carnations, celery, water, ink, yoghurt pots
food colouring

THE 'WHAT TO DO WITH THE STUFF' BIT

Get a few jars or yoghurt pots. Put some water into the
bottom of each one. Add a few drops of ink to one, different

97

coloured ink to another, food colouring to yet another, and mark on the outside what you've added to the pot. Using white flowers like carnations, put some long stemmed and some short stemmed flowers into the various pots and wait to see what happens. After a day the short stemmed flowers will start to change colour. The long stemmed ones will take a little longer. You can see why by sticking some celery into one of the pots. If you cut it across you can see how much the water has been sucked up through the veins.

Next split the stem of a new carnation in half to just under the flower head. Then, stand one half of the stem in one coloured pot and the other half in a different coloured pot. The flower will change into two different colours. Have a

good fiddle with the flowers and inks and yoghurt pots and you can maybe make some very loud and colourful flowers.

THE 'HEY BRILLIANT, IT WORKS' BIT

If you've marked the pots, you should see that the ink makes the whole flower change colour, but the food colouring changes only the ends of the petals. Interesting, eh? Just see how crazy you can make the flowers look.

THE 'O.K., HOW DOES IT WORK?' BIT

Now, plants and flowers suck up water through their roots and stems to feed the leaves and petals. Plants have roots which go deep into the soil so that they can reach water which is well below the surface. The water contains things called minerals which the plants need to make food, so roots are essential to keep the plants alive. You can't normally see plants sucking up water through roots and stems but by adding the ink it's quite clear. If you've done the bit with the celery, then you can see how short stemmed flowers change colour quicker than those with long stems. It just takes less time for the coloured water to reach the flower head.

CRYSTAL BALLS

THE 'STUFF YOU NEED' BIT

Washing soda, or Epsom salts

Pencil, string, a length of wool, saucer, glasses,
food colouring

THE 'WHAT TO DO WITH THE STUFF' BIT

Bring four cupfuls of water to the boil in a pan. Plonk in
washing soda or Epsom salts until you can't make any more
dissolve in the water. When that happens, you've got the
mixture just right. Let it cool off in the pan before you do
anything more with it.

Tie a crystal of washing soda on to one end of a piece of
string and tie the other end to the middle of a pencil. Fill a
glass with the mixture and lie the pencil across the top so
that the washing soda crystal is hanging in the middle.
Leave it for a few hours (or even longer) and watch the
crystal grow.

Put a few drops of food colouring into another glass and pour the mixture on top. Mix it up a bit. Hang a length of thick wool into the mixture with a bit hanging over the top of the glass. Leave that for a few hours, and see what colour crystals you get this time.

Pour a little bit of the mixture into a flat saucer or plate and leave it for a few days. Crystals grow beautifully and the longer you leave them, the bigger and more beautiful they become.

THE 'HEY BRILLIANT, IT WORKS' BIT

You can make a crystal garden with a bit more effort. Make a mixture of two tablespoons of salt and two of washing soda in some hot water. Put some little pieces of coal, coke or cinders into a tray and pour the mixture on top. Then put some iodine (in drops) around the garden. Leave it for a few days and see what happens.

THE 'O.K., HOW DOES IT WORK?' BIT

Crystals are solid substances which have a regular shape. Lots of things around the house are crystals, like salt, sugar, sand, bath salts and washing soda. When you put them in water, particularly hot water, they dissolve to form a mixture called a 'solution'. So a salt solution is just water with a load of salt in it, or a washing soda solution is water with a load of washing soda in it.

To get the salt or the washing soda out of the water you can use all sorts of different ways. The mixture in the saucer 'evaporated', that is, all the water disappeared, leaving behind lots of crystals. This is how sugar is made. Sugar cane is mashed up and mixed with water to dissolve the sugar. The sugar solution is sieved away from the stalks and then left to evaporate. What's left is sugar.

POP THE CORN – WELL, SOMETIMES

THE 'STUFF YOU NEED' BIT

Popping corn

Big saucepan with a lid

THE 'WHAT TO DO WITH THE STUFF' BIT

Sorry – got to have another adult to help with this one.

Have you ever popped corn before? No? Well, it's really loud and brilliant. Put about three tablespoons of oil in the bottom of a big saucepan, heat it up until it starts to smoke, and then throw in about half a cupful of popping corn. Put the lid on quickly otherwise you will have corn everywhere. The corn explodes inside the pan. Take the pan off the heat and wait until all the popping has stopped. It's amazing how much the corn changes in size. If you like sweet popcorn mix it up with some syrup, and it's sticky and gorgeous.

Next, put about a cupful of fresh popping corn into the oven, set at a low heat, for about an hour and a half: this will dry the corn out. Then do exactly the same thing to pop it using the big saucepan as you did with the fresh popping corn. See what happens.

Finally, leave some corn in water overnight. Drain it off and pop it in the pan like before. See what happens. How much of the three types of corn pops, and what size is the popped corn? Keep a little bowl of each type to compare it.

THE 'HEY BRILLIANT, IT WORKS' BIT

Make a note of the different sizes of popped corn, measure it if you like with a rule. The fresh corn should be the biggest, then the dried corn, and finally the horrible watered corn.

THE 'O.K., HOW DOES IT WORK?' BIT

Popping corn is just a special type of seed and although it looks dry, it still contains a bit of water. This little bit of water keeps the seed alive inside until it's put into soil to start sprouting. Now when a kernel of popping corn is heated quickly, the water inside it turns into steam. The steam builds up inside and when the pressure is big enough, the steam bursts through the hard shell. POP, POP, POP, POP – that is the pop in popcorn. As the steam is on its way out, it puffs up the softer material inside the seed to give popcorn its very special puffed up shape.

Now, when you dry out the corn in the oven a lot of the water inside the shell disappears. So when it's heated there may not be enough steam to pop the corn. If you've dried it out enough, some of the corn won't pop. The corn which

does pop, has less steam inside it to puff the softer bits out and so the popcorn will be smaller than usual.

When you soak the corn beforehand, the hard shell softens and allows water to get inside. When the water turns into steam, it breaks through the soft shell very easily and the corn doesn't turn into popcorn at all.

MAKE YOUR OWN FIRE EXTINGUISHER

THE 'STUFF YOU NEED' BIT

White vinegar

Bicarbonate of soda

Candle

THE 'WHAT TO DO WITH THE STUFF' BIT

Sorry – got to have an adult to help with the matches.

Put a teaspoon of bicarbonate of soda in a glass and pour on two centimetres of vinegar. Mix it all together and you'll see bubbles rising up the glass. Light the candle and then tip the glass as if you're emptying the mixture over the flame, but don't let any of the mixture out. The candle will go out.

THE 'HEY BRILLIANT, IT WORKS' BIT

You could also put the same mixture in a bottle. Put a straw through a cork and push the cork into the bottle. Now turn it upside down and the gas will come out of the straw. Sometimes, if you do it quickly, the gas will shoot through the straw, just like a real fire extinguisher.

THE 'O.K., HOW DOES IT WORK?' BIT

When the vinegar and the bicarbonate of soda are mixed together they form a gas called 'carbon dioxide'. Now carbon dioxide is heavier than the air which we breathe, so when you mix the vinegar and bicarbonate of soda together, this special gas stays inside the glass.

For a flame to keep burning it needs to have a gas called 'oxygen' around it. When you tip the glass over the candle, you are flooding the flame with carbon dioxide – it is starved of oxygen and goes out. Firemen sometimes use extinguishers which spray a foam full of carbon dioxide bubbles onto the flames. Just like our trick with the candle, the flames are starved of oxygen and go out.

CRUNCHY FROTHY TOFFEE

THE 'STUFF YOU NEED' BIT

Golden syrup

Sugar

Bicarbonate of soda (but not Baking Powder, which isn't the same thing)

A dish about four centimetres deep

Large saucepan

THE 'WHAT TO DO WITH THE STUFF' BIT

You will need a grown up to help you with this one. Using a large saucepan, put in four tablespoons of sugar and two tablespoons of golden syrup, bring them to the boil and then simmer for five minutes. The toffee will turn dark brown in the pan. Watch this next bit really carefully because it's fantastic. Put a heaped teaspoon of bicarbonate of soda into the toffee and stir it round really quickly – watch it turn into a huge, orange frothy crunchy goo. Pour it into a greased dish and wait for it to cool. If you like gooey sweets, coat it in chocolate and eat loads of it.

THE 'HEY BRILLIANT, IT WORKS' BIT

Try mixing bicarbonate of soda with lemon squash or orange squash and see if it fizzes.

THE 'O.K., HOW DOES IT WORK?' BIT

When you boil the sugar and the syrup together they caramelise (melt) and eventually turn into dark brown toffee. When you add the bicarbonate of soda, carbon dioxide is formed and bubbles up inside the toffee. It bubbles up so much that the whole mixture becomes frothy and orange. It's the carbon dioxide which does the whole trick.

TEST YOUR TASTES

THE 'STUFF YOU NEED' BIT

Your tongue!

Sugar, salt, coffee, lemon juice, vinegar

THE 'WHAT TO DO WITH THE STUFF' BIT

There are four different parts to your tongue and each one can detect certain things. One part tells you what is sweet, another bitter, another salty and the last one sour.

To test the different areas, get a friend to help you. The more people who do this, the better. Start off by dabbing a little bit of sugar on the front of your tongue, what does it taste like? Next dab some sugar right at the back of your tongue. What is the difference? Finally, try sugar on the right side of your tongue and then on the left side. Is there any difference? Then swill your mouth out with water and do exactly the same thing with the sour vinegar or lemon juice. Rinse again and then taste the bitter coffee and finally, the salt. Make notes of what tastes best on different parts of the tongue. Draw a tongue and mark it out on a piece of paper.

THE 'HEY BRILLIANT, IT WORKS' BIT

It's better still if you hold your nose when you're doing it.

Try pinching your nose and eating some food. Does it taste normal? It shouldn't.

THE 'O.K., HOW DOES IT WORK?' BIT

Your tongue should show four main areas of taste. The front of your tongue can taste sweet and salty things; the back can taste bitter things only; both the left and the right hand side can taste sour and sweet things. The areas do overlap a bit but the main areas should show up.

When you've got a cold and your nose is blocked up, it's hard to taste food properly. That's because the smell of the food is very important to us. When we can't smell the food we rely totally on our taste buds on our tongue. So if you have to take some horrible medicine or eat horrid things, hold your nose and they won't taste half as bad.

ROLF HARRIS

YOUR CARTOON TIME

Did you know that you can draw?

Rolf Harris shows you how – clearly and simply – in
YOUR CARTOON TIME. Starting with stick figures,
he explains how to develop these step-by-step into
your own stylish characters, and there are ideas too
for how you can use your drawings – as birthday
cards, home movies and so on.

DRAWING IS FUN!

All you need is a pencil, paper and Rolf Harris's book
– YOUR CARTOON TIME.

KNIGHT BOOKS